SHAKESPEARE FOR EVERYONE

OTHELLO

By Jennifer Mulherin and Abigail Frost
Illustrations by Jonathon Heap
CHERRYTREE BOOKS

Author's note

There is no substitute for seeing the plays of Shakespeare performed. Only then can you really understand why Shakespeare is our greatest dramatist and poet. This book simply gives you the background to the play and tells you about the story and characters. It will, I hope, encourage you to see the play.

A Cherrytree Book

Designed and produced by
A S Publishing

First published 1990
by Cherrytree Press Ltd
327 High Street
Slough
Berkshire SL1 1TX

Reprinted 1999, 2001

Copyright this edition © Evans Brothers Ltd 2001

British Library Cataloguing in Publication Data
Mulherin, Jennifer
    Othello
    I. Title II. Series III Frost, Abigail.
    822.3'3

ISBN 1 84234 034 4

Printed in Hong Kong through Colorcraft Ltd

Contents

Othello *and the soldier's life*

In 1588, the Spanish Armada sailed to invade England, but like the Turkish fleet in Othello, *it met foul weather, and the ships were scattered.*

Shakespeare probably wrote *Othello* in 1604. There was a new king, James I, on the throne, and perhaps he was inspired to try something new. In any case, *Othello* is unusual among his tragedies. Its leading characters are not kings and queens or great figures from history, but army officers and their wives, from Shakespeare's own time. No empires fall because of Othello's sad fate; the 'tragedy' rests in the terrible results of jealousy.

Shakespeare took his plot from a novel by an Italian author, Cinthio, which was published in 1566. A French translation was published about 20 years later, but it was not translated into English in Shakespeare's lifetime.

The tragedy of Othello and Desdemona is a tragedy set in a small, closed community – the 'officers' mess' of Othello's army. For most of the play, the characters are living on the island of Cyprus. They have defeated the Turkish army that they came to fight at sea, and they have little to occupy their minds. Gossip and personal jealousies are bound to flourish in such an atmosphere; not only about love-affairs, but about army life itself. Who has been promoted, and why? Who has suddenly fallen out of favour? How can a man catch the commander's eye?

Shakespeare's audience would have found the scene familiar. The court of Elizabeth I (who died the year before the play was written) buzzed with similar intrigues. And many spectators would have experienced the soldier's life directly. The English had recently been fighting the Spanish in the Netherlands, and Lord Mountjoy had just defeated a rebellion in Ireland.

Memories of England's greatest sea-battle, against the Spanish Armada, would have been stirred by Othello's triumphant landing on Cyprus. Even those who had been small children at the time would remember the soldiers mustering, or seeing the Queen sail down the Thames to review her troops at Tilbury.

How to handle cannon, from The Four Books of Chivalry *(1529). Firearms had to be cleaned and reloaded after each shot, which took a long time. But they required less skill than bows and arrows to be fired with lethal effect.*

An impoverished army

Elizabeth's army was conscripted on a county-by-county basis. Each Lord Lieutenant was expected to supply a certain number of men and weapons. Musters were held when forces were needed. The Queen paid for the wars, but commanders frequently had to pay soldiers' wages and reclaim the money.

A good general, like Othello, would have seen that his men were well-trained, disciplined, and well looked after; but to serve under a bad general could mean near-starvation. An officer's unit was seen almost as his property. Recruitment, training and promotion were very much in his hands, with no central control. One English commander in the 1580s even sold his troops to the Spaniards!

Similarly, hungry soldiers might sell their weapons and gunpowder; a double danger, since not only were they now unarmed, but usually the final customer was the enemy.

The idea of a national army, controlled by the government of the day, finally came to England with Cromwell's organization of the parliamentary troops to fight the Civil War of 1642-46.

'The fiery weapons'

Armies were changing fast in Shakespeare's time. By about 1560, shortly before he was born, the English had finally abandoned the longbow in favour of firearms. But many people looked back to the days of the bowmen with regret. Writing in 1598, Robert Barret tells how a gentleman complained to a captain that the longbow had served the English well enough in the past. 'Sir, then was then and now is now. The wars are much altered since the fiery weapons first came up.'

Strangely, guns are hardly mentioned in *Othello*. The cannons are fired to welcome the new general, and that is all. If we are to judge by his last speech, Othello preferred to fight with his sword – and to die upon it.

Square-bashers and arithmeticians

Another innovation was drill. 'Square-bashing' has been a daily routine for soldiers for so long that it is hard to imagine an army without it. Again, it would have been up to

Discipline was slack amongst 'soldiers of fortune'. Often commanders cheated them out of their pay and they went hungry, so they took to looting. This mercenary has bagged himself a fowl.

5

individual officers to introduce drill; they learnt how from books of military theory. These books gave ideas for fortress designs and battle formations, and taught readers how to survey a battlefield. The new style of officer had to understand some mathematics.

One of the first books of this kind in English was *An Arithmetical Warlike Treatise named Stratioticos*, by Thomas Digges (1579). As well as drill, Digges taught his readers fractions and equations. He believed English soldiers needed a modern disciplinary system, and admired the Spanish, because 'of all the other nations there is none more obedient to their officers'. The 'best gentleman or nobleman' in a Spanish unit would obey orders from a common sergeant – unlike his English equivalent.

Iago complains that Cassio is 'a great arithmetician' – something of an accountant (not to be scorned, given the commander's problem of paying the soldiers and reclaiming the money later), but also a man who has learned about war as much from books like Digges's as from experience.

Digges's complaints about discipline seem to have been well-founded. Elizabethan officers writing home often mention drunken fights among their men, or even with local allies. In this respect, Othello's Venetian soldiers seem thoroughly English.

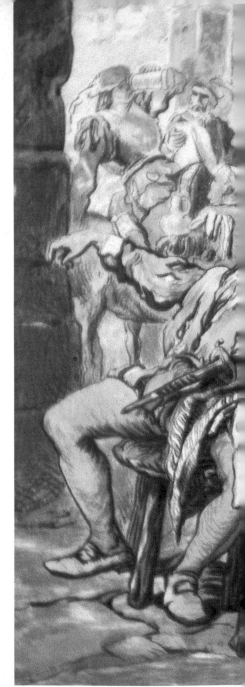

Drunkenness and brawling were a nightly occurrence. Against his better judgement, Cassio was persuaded to join in the merriment by Iago's catchy song:
  'And let me the canakin clink, clink;'

A Moor in Venice

The full title of the play is *The Tragedy of Othello, the Moor of Venice*, although most of it is set in Cyprus. But knowing the history of this Italian city helps us understand the play. What, after all, was a man from Africa doing leading an Italian army in Cyprus?

From the Middle Ages until the mid-1700s, Venice was the centre of a great trading empire. It was ruled by a council of senators (like Brabantio), whose leader was the Doge (or Duke, translated into English). The Venetians were the descendants of people who fled from barbarian invaders when the Roman Empire collapsed. They settled on islands in a lagoon on the Adriatic Sea, and over the centuries, extended the islands and created new, artificial ones, on which they built one of the greatest cities of the world.

They had little room to grow food, and naturally turned to trade to support themselves. Spices, rich silk cloth, precious stones and all manner of luxury goods passed in and out of the Venetian merchants' warehouses, bringing great wealth to the citizens. Trade in turn provoked disputes with other countries – which meant the Venetians needed fighting ships, and fighting men.

Turkey and Cyprus

The other great Mediterranean sea-power was Turkey, which held the key to the riches of the East. The Venetians were often at war with the Turks. From 1489 to 1573, they ruled the island of Cyprus, not far from the Turkish coast. Cyprus was enormously important to both sides, since whoever controlled it had a secure base in the East Mediterranean. (Even today it is one of the Royal Navy's most important bases.)

It was fashionable to have a black servant in a fine uniform. Perhaps the black gondolier in this painting by Carpaccio was the 'chauffeur' of a rich Venetian merchant.

The Turks decided to fight this Venetian threat on their doorstep in 1570, and the Venetians finally surrendered all rights to it three years later. Although Othello's victory cannot be matched to any real battle in this war, it is obvious that the play is set during it.

Black people in Italy

It is not really very surprising that an African should have ended up working for the Venetians. Venice had a small population compared with its enemies, so it hired foreign mercenaries, or 'soldiers of fortune', to fill up the army. And Venice was visited by people of many different countries.

Tourists in Venice today can see *The Miracle of the True Cross at the Rialto*, a painting by Carpaccio, who worked a hundred years before Shakespeare. It is a bustling scene of daily life, which includes a black gondolier rowing across the Grand Canal. If he could find his way there from Africa, so could Othello.

Othello's roots

But where, exactly, did Othello come from? Shakespeare often shows himself to be ignorant of geography. The word 'moor' means, strictly, someone from Mauritania in North Africa – and the people there are of Arabic descent. But Shakespeare obviously imagined him as a true black African from further south.

Shakespeare would not have been taught much about other countries at school. He lived in an age when few people owned maps of the world, unless, like sea-captains or merchants, they needed them for work. He may only have had a vague idea that black people came from Africa (with no notion of how vast and varied the continent really is), and used the word 'moor' to describe anyone from there with a dark skin.

A painting called Two Negroes *by Rembrandt. Though Shakespeare calls Othello a 'moor', he probably saw him as a black African rather than as an Arab.*

The African connection

A few black Africans lived in Shakespeare's London, which was a great port like Venice. Many came as sailors via Portugal, or the Arab lands of North Africa and the Middle East. The Arabs travelled as far south as Zimbabwe to trade goods. They brought people back with them – sometimes as slaves to be sold, sometimes as extra hands for the voyage.

Africans who travelled to Europe at this time would probably never go home again. Many stayed on at sea as sailors. Some married locally and settled down to ordinary jobs. And some, like Othello, joined the mercenary armies of Europe, ready to fight and die for any ruler who would pay them well.

The story of Othello

Late one night in the city of Venice, two men approach the house of Senator Brabantio. Iago, a soldier, and Roderigo, a vain young gentleman, rouse the old man with shouts. 'Look to your house, your daughter and your bags! Thieves! Thieves!'.

At his window, the senator tells them to stop their drunken noise. He has refused to let Roderigo marry his daughter, Desdemona, and will not change his mind. Iago says they have bad news: Desdemona has eloped with his general, Othello, a Moor who serves the city for pay.

Iago has a reason for telling Brabantio. He is bitter because Othello has chosen Cassio as his lieutenant, giving Iago the lower rank of 'ancient' or ensign.

But for now, Iago must seem loyal. He goes to warn Othello that Brabantio is coming. Othello is not worried: the

Iago's false face
Though I do hate him as I do hell-pains,
Yet, for necessity of present life,
I must show out a flag and sign of love,
Which is indeed but sign.

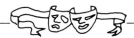

Act I Sci

Othello calms Brabantio
Keep up your bright swords,
for the dew will rust
them.
Good signior, you shall
more command with
years
Than with your weapons.

Act I Scii

Duke of Venice will not arrest his best general over such a trifle. Cassio arrives to summon Othello to the Duke's council chamber; after him comes Brabantio, with Roderigo and some soldiers.

Witchcraft

Brabantio draws his sword, but Othello softly refuses his

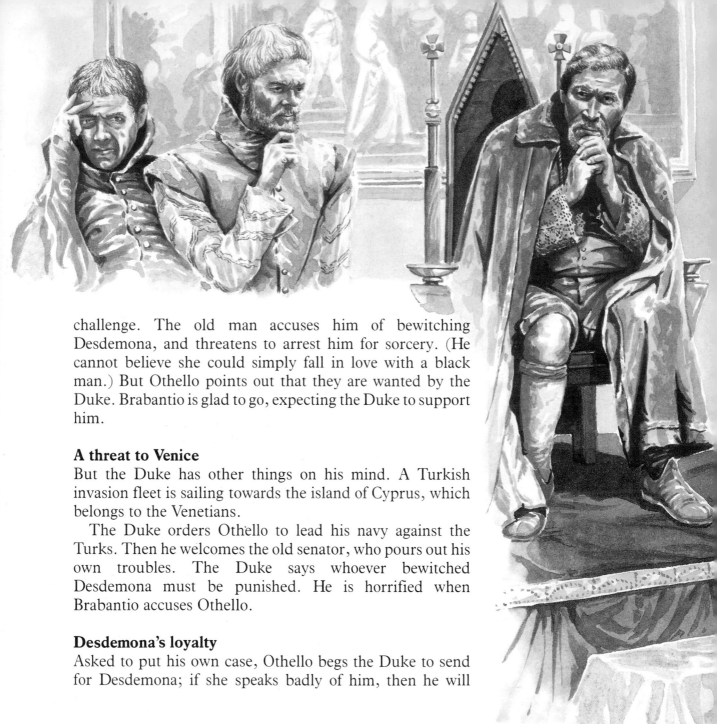

challenge. The old man accuses him of bewitching Desdemona, and threatens to arrest him for sorcery. (He cannot believe she could simply fall in love with a black man.) But Othello points out that they are wanted by the Duke. Brabantio is glad to go, expecting the Duke to support him.

A threat to Venice

But the Duke has other things on his mind. A Turkish invasion fleet is sailing towards the island of Cyprus, which belongs to the Venetians.

The Duke orders Othello to lead his navy against the Turks. Then he welcomes the old senator, who pours out his own troubles. The Duke says whoever bewitched Desdemona must be punished. He is horrified when Brabantio accuses Othello.

Desdemona's loyalty

Asked to put his own case, Othello begs the Duke to send for Desdemona; if she speaks badly of him, then he will

14

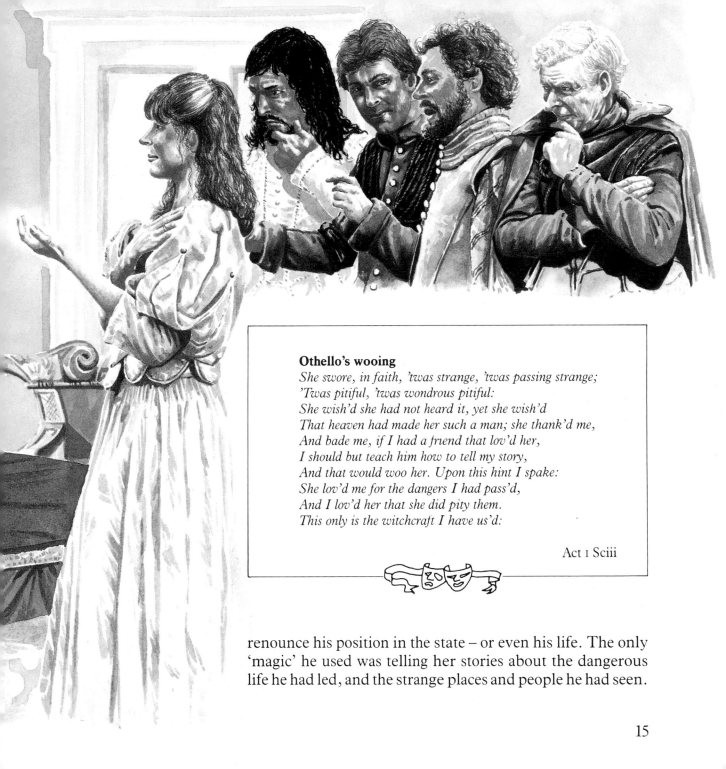

Othello's wooing

She swore, in faith, 'twas strange, 'twas passing strange;
'Twas pitiful, 'twas wondrous pitiful:
She wish'd she had not heard it, yet she wish'd
That heaven had made her such a man; she thank'd me,
And bade me, if I had a friend that lov'd her,
I should but teach him how to tell my story,
And that would woo her. Upon this hint I spake:
She lov'd me for the dangers I had pass'd,
And I lov'd her that she did pity them.
This only is the witchcraft I have us'd:

Act I Sciii

renounce his position in the state – or even his life. The only
'magic' he used was telling her stories about the dangerous
life he had led, and the strange places and people he had seen.

15

Iago brings Desdemona to the Duke. She says she loves and respects her father, but now her duty is to her husband. Brabantio, realising he has lost, bitterly accepts the situation. The Duke orders Othello to get ready to leave for Cyprus.

Roderigo is distressed that Desdemona is married. Iago says she will not love her husband long, and suggests that Roderigo can lure her away with money. But Iago is only thinking of himself, and revenge on Othello.

A victorious landing

The scene shifts to Cyprus. The island's governor, Montano, is anxiously looking out to sea. Othello's fleet, helped by a storm, has seen off the Turks; but can the Venetians land safely? One by one the ships arrive, and their commanders come to Montano; first Cassio, and then Iago, who brings his wife Emilia, Roderigo, and the beautiful Desdemona.

Lovers' greetings?

The courteous Cassio greets Desdemona with flowery compliments, and kisses her hand. Iago takes notice – this will help his plot against Othello. Trumpets sound a fanfare: Othello's ship has landed safely. Iago laughs to see Desdemona welcome him with a kiss.

As everyone moves on, Iago and Roderigo talk. Iago says Desdemona is obviously tiring of Othello, and has fallen in love with Cassio. After all, she encouraged him to kiss her hand! Roderigo finds it hard to believe, but Iago presses on. He suggests Roderigo get Cassio into trouble by starting a fight with him. With Cassio out of the way, perhaps Desdemona will fall for him.

A devious plot

On his own, Iago reveals his plan for revenge. He will drive Othello mad with jealousy.

Desdemona's plea

*I saw Othello's visage in
  his mind,
And to his honours and his
  valiant parts
Did I my soul and fortunes
  consecrate.
So that, dear lords, if I be
  left behind,
A moth of peace, and he
  go to the war,
The rites for which I love
  him are bereft me,
And I a heavy interim
  shall support
By his dear absence.
Let me go with him.*

Act I Sciii

Cassio greets Desdemona
*   O! behold,
The riches of the ship is
  come on shore.
Ye men of Cyprus, let her
  have your knees.
Hail to thee, lady! and the
  grace of heaven,
Before, behind thee, and on
  every hand,
Enwheel thee round!*

Act II Sci

Iago's chance comes that night. He and Cassio are waiting to go on guard, during a festival to celebrate Othello's wedding and his victory. At first, Cassio refuses a drink – he has a weak head. But soon Iago has everyone singing drinking songs. Cassio forgets his resolution, and drinks along with the rest – just as Iago planned.

Cassio's disgrace

The drunken lieutenant staggers off. Iago sends Roderigo after him. Soon he returns at the point of Cassio's sword. Montano tries to part them, but Cassio fights him off. Othello, roused by the noise, is disgusted to see his lieutenant in such a state – and fighting with the governor of Cyprus!

Iago pretends to be reluctant to accuse Cassio, but his account is all the more damning for that. Othello believes every word. 'Cassio, I love thee,' he says, 'But never more be officer of mine.'

Poisoned advice

Cassio, sobering up, asks Iago for advice. Iago suggests he ask Desdemona to plead his case; Othello will refuse her nothing. (Perhaps he will also wonder why she is so keen to have Cassio reinstated, thinks Iago.) Next morning Cassio comes to Iago's house and easily charms Emilia into talking to Desdemona on his behalf.

As soon as she is asked, Desdemona promises to help. Othello and Iago appear, and Cassio hastily leaves. (Once again, he plays into Iago's hands.) 'Was not that Cassio parted from my wife?' asks Othello. Iago says it cannot be – 'No, sure, I cannot think it, that he would steal away so guilty-like, seeing you coming.' Iago's 'defence' shows Cassio in the worst possible light.

Innocent Desdemona at once begs her husband to forgive Cassio. 'Not now, sweet Desdemona; some other time', he says, but she persists. At last Othello wavers a little;

> **Desdemona promises her help**
> *My lord shall never rest;*
> *I'll watch him tame, and talk him out of patience;*
> *His bed shall seem a school, his board a shrift;*
> *I'll intermingle every thing he does*
> *With Cassio's suit.*
> *Therefore be merry, Cassio;*
>
> Act III Sciii

> **Jealousy stirs**
> *O curse of marriage!*
> *That we can call these delicate creatures ours,*
> *And not their appetites. I had rather be a toad,*
> *And live upon the vapour of a dungeon,*
> *Than keep a corner in the thing I love*
> *For others' uses.*
>
> Act III Sciii

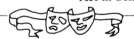

Desdemona, satisfied for now, leaves him, and Iago sets to work to raise suspicion. He suggests that Othello should keep a watch on his wife and Cassio. He goes, leaving Othello in terrible distress.

The fatal handkerchief

Desdemona and Emilia return. As soon as Othello sees his wife, he cries out, unable to believe she is untrue to him. She rushes to his side and asks if he is ill. He says he has a headache, and she tries to bandage his head with her embroidered handkerchief – but it is too small and she lets it drop to the ground.

Othello demands proof

By the world,
I think my wife be honest
and think she is not;
I think that thou art just
and think thou art not.
I'll have some proof. Her
name, that was as fresh
As Dian's visage, is now
begrim'd and black
As mine own face. If there
be cords or knives,
Poison or fire or suffocating
streams,
I'll not endure it. Would I
were satisfied!

Act III Sciii

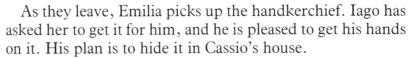

As they leave, Emilia picks up the handkerchief. Iago has asked her to get it for him, and he is pleased to get his hands on it. His plan is to hide it in Cassio's house.

Othello returns, unable to decide what to think. He cannot bear the uncertainty, and must have proof of his wife's unfaithfulness. Iago says he saw Cassio wipe his beard with Desdemona's handkerchief. The horrified general orders Iago to kill Cassio. Iago says it will be done – 'but let her live'. In this way, he puts the most terrible idea of all into Othello's mind.

Othello wants to find out if Desdemona still has the handkerchief, which once belonged to his mother. He asks to borrow it, saying he has a cold; but of course she has not got it. He becomes angry when she denies losing it, and she makes it worse by trying to distract him by talking about Cassio. He leaves in a rage.

> **The fatal handkerchief**
> *That handkerchief*
> *Did an Egyptian to my*
> *   mother give; . . .*
> *. . . She dying gave it me;*
> *And bid me, when my fate*
> *   would have me wive,*
> *To give it her. I did so: and*
> *   take heed on't;*
> *Make it a darling like your*
> *   precious eye;*
> *To lose't or give't away,*
> *   were such perdition*
> *As nothing else could*
> *   match.*
>
> Act III Sc iv

A woman scorned

Desdemona sadly tells Cassio that things are not going well; Othello is angry with her, and will not listen to her pleas. As she leaves, another woman comes to talk to Cassio – Bianca, a prostitute who is in love with him.

Bianca is upset because Cassio has not been to see her. He asks her to forgive him, then, astonishingly, gives her Desdemona's handkerchief. He has found it in his house, and likes the design; will Bianca sew him a copy? She naturally thinks another woman has given it to him, but she agrees to meet him later.

Othello loses control

Iago continues to torment Othello, who is now half-mad with jealousy, and completely in his power. He talks incoherently about honour, lust – and the handkerchief. At last he falls down into a fit.

While he is unconscious, Cassio comes, but Iago sends him away for a moment. Othello recovers; Iago tells him Cassio has been there, and suggests that he should listen to their conversation when he returns.

Mistaken conclusions

Iago and Cassio gossip about Bianca, mocking this pathetic woman. 'She gives it out that you shall marry her!' Cassio laughs at the very idea. But Othello thinks it is his wife they are discussing so crudely. Bianca herself arrives, thrusting Desdemona's handkerchief back into Cassio's hand. 'This is some minx's token!' Iago could not have hoped for better luck. Cassio runs off after Bianca.

Othello in the depths

Now Othello has murder on his mind. 'Get me some poison, Iago!' Iago says it would be better to strangle her on her marriage-bed. Othello agrees, but as they talk Desdemona interrupts, bringing Lodovico, a Venetian gentleman with a letter from the Duke.

While he reads the letter, a summons back to Venice, Desdemona talks to Lodovico. Suddenly Othello turns round, shouts at her and hits her. Horrified, Lodovico asks if the letter has made him angry; but Iago hints that the general is mad.

At home, Othello questions Emilia about his wife's behaviour, and sends her to fetch Desdemona so that they can talk alone. He makes his terrible accusation to the poor, bewildered girl: 'Heaven truly knows that thou art false as hell.' The more she pleads innocence, the more angry he becomes.

Poor Desdemona confides in Emilia and Iago; she cannot see what she has done to provoke such jealousy. Emilia tries to console her.

Iago turns the screw
Do but encave yourself,
And mark the fleers, the
gibes, and notable
scorns,
That dwell in every region
of his face;
For I will make him tell the
tale anew,
Where, how, how oft, how
long ago, and when
He hath, and is again to
cope your wife:
I say, but mark his gesture.

Act IV Sci

Murderous thoughts
Ay, let her rot, and perish,
and be damned to-night; for
she shall not live. No, my
heart is turned to stone; I
strike it, and it hurts my
hand. O! the world hath
not a sweeter creature; she
might lie by an emperor's
side and command him
tasks.

Act IV Sci

Roderigo's jewels

As the ladies leave for supper, Roderigo confronts Iago. Iago had promised to win Desdemona for him, by giving her presents of jewels; now he is sick of waiting, and wants the jewels back. Of course, the jewels never reached her – Iago kept them for himself.

Iago retrieves this awkward situation by telling Roderigo that Othello has been recalled by the Duke. Only an unforeseen event, such as an 'accident' befalling Cassio might make him stay. Roderigo will have an opportunity to kill Cassio when he visits Bianca.

A duel in the street

Iago wants to get rid of both Cassio and Roderigo. He is still consumed with jealousy of the charming lieutenant, and he does not want to repay Roderigo for the presents he was supposed to have sent. He hopes that one will kill the other, and be hanged for murder.

He waits with Roderigo in the dark street. When Cassio appears, Roderigo stabs ineffectually at him. Cassio strikes back and wounds him. In the darkness, Iago stabs Cassio, who falls to the ground. Othello enters, thinking Iago has kept his promise to kill Cassio. He leaves to carry out his own dreadful plan.

Lodovico and his companion Gratiano arrive; Cassio revives and calls out for help – and so does Roderigo. In the confusion, Iago kills Roderigo.

Desdemona's last hour

Othello enters Desdemona's bedroom, determined that she shall die. When he sees her, he cannot bear to shed her blood, and kisses her for the last time; but he still believes that justice demands that she die. She wakes, and he asks if she has said her prayers.

Othello tells his wife to pray for forgiveness. When she asks him to explain, he accuses her of giving her handkerchief to Cassio. At last Desdemona realises that she and Cassio have been innocent victims of a plot – but the more she cries out, the more determined Othello becomes. She begs piteously for time – a day, half an hour, time to say a prayer; but Othello smothers her with a pillow.

Emilia rushes in. As she tells Othello the news of Roderigo's death, Desdemona cries out with her dying breath. 'O, who has done this deed?' asks Emilia. 'Nobody; I myself,' says Desdemona, and dies.

The truth comes out

Emilia turns on Othello in anger and distress. He confesses that he killed Desdemona, explaining that Iago had proved she was false. Emilia shouts at him in contempt, and calls for help. Montano, Iago and others come running. Iago says he only told Othello what he believed to be true. As the accusations fly, Othello mentions the handkerchief. Emilia, realising what has been going on, tells him she took the handkerchief and gave it to Iago.

Iago attacks his wife, who has such damning evidence against him, and kills her. He escapes, but Montano and his men run after him and arrest him.

At last Othello knows the dreadful truth. He finds his favourite sword, and stabs Iago, but is prevented from killing him. While the others untangle the whole story, he is lost in thought. Lodovico arrests him for the murder of Desdemona, and he asks to speak.

A final kiss

Othello asks that the others 'speak of me as I am'; they must not try to excuse what he has done, or make him out to be a terrible villain. Then he talks of a long-ago battle, when he killed a Turk; as he speaks of stabbing his enemy, he stabs himself. He falls on the bed beside the lifeless Desdemona, and dies kissing her.

Othello's last words
When you shall these unlucky deeds relate,
Speak of me as I am; nothing extenuate,
Nor set down aught in malice: then, must you speak
Of one that lov'd not wisely but too well;

Act v Scii

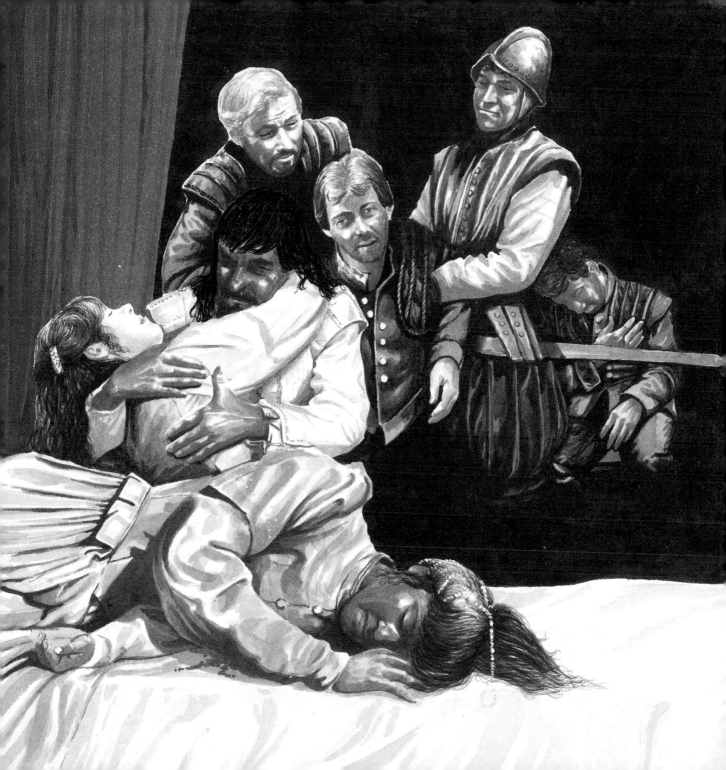

The play's characters

Othello

Iago's view of Othello
The Moor is of a free and open nature,
That thinks men honest that but seem to be so,
And will as tenderly be led by the nose
As asses are.

Act I Sciii

Othello

O! now, for ever
Farewell the tranquil mind;
*   farewell content!*

Act III Sciii

When we first meet Othello we cannot help but be impressed by his dignity and good sense. With gentle humour, he prevents a fight, calming the angry Brabantio without ridiculing him. At the Duke's council meeting, we learn something of his adventurous past. He is evidently a soldier worthy of the Duke's trust. In Cyprus, he shows his dislike of uncontrolled behaviour when he dismisses Cassio for a drunken brawl. But, when his own feelings are in question, he too easily loses control of himself. Iago plays quite cruelly on his deepest insecurities, especially the fear that, as a foreigner and a simple soldier, the sophisticated Venetians will laugh at him. He loves Desdemona so much that he cannot bear to lose her – and once the seeds of suspicion are sown, the terror turns into rage and he becomes literally mad with jealousy. Once Emilia has spoken, and revealed Iago's lies for what they are, he quickly sees how he has been deceived. But Desdemona is dead, and it is too late; Othello's only solution is to die himself.

Desdemona

Desdemona shows herself when she first appears as a brave young woman. Having heard so much about the wars from Othello, she wants to see them for herself, and insists on coming to Cyprus with the army. But once she is there, safely married to the man she loves, she never thinks that anything could go wrong until it is too late. She does not know, as we do, how Iago is twisting Othello's feelings, but she is tactless when she insists on pressing Cassio's case when Othello obviously does not want to listen. As he becomes more and more angry with her, she simply cannot understand what is happening. Yet she remains loyal to the end, bravely hiding her feelings when the Venetian lords arrive to summon Othello home, and even, with her dying breath, trying to take all the blame herself.

Iago

Desdemona

Iago

Iago is a typical villain of Jacobean drama – a cold, cunning type who presents a false face to the world. He is known to the world as 'honest Iago', ever-ready with good advice, a drink or a joke. But under this cover he robs Rodrigo, plots the downfall of Cassio, and deliberately drives Othello to murder to punish him for promoting Cassio instead of himself. He is quick to spot others' weaknesses – Cassio's weak head for liquor, as well as Othello's insecurity. He has an eye for jealousy especially, because he is himself both envious and jealous. People fatally trust him because he seems an unsophisticated man of action, yet underneath he is highly intelligent, able to make devious plans and change them quickly to take advantage of any new situation. He might have made a good general himself, if only he had turned his mind away from his own advantage.

Cassio

Rodrigo

Emilia

Emilia

I care not for thy sword;
I'll make thee known,
Though I lost twenty lives.

Act V Scii

Emilia really is 'honest' – she speaks her mind freely, and nothing will stop her revealing the truth about the handkerchief at the end. She is kind and reassuring to Desdemona when her mistress is in the depths of misery. But, like Desdemona, she does not see what is going on under her nose. When she finds the handkerchief, she never asks why Iago should want such a thing, but simply takes it to please him. Though she must know her husband better than anyone, she does not recognise him for the villain he is until his plans have reached their tragic conclusion.

Cassio

A typical Renaissance courtier, Cassio is charming, intelligent and capable. He and Iago do not understand each other. He is puzzled by Iago's crude humour. Iago sees his courtly treatment of Desdemona and Emilia as lustful advances. He tries to get Othello to forgive him his disgrace in the proper courtly manner, sending messages through Desdemona, but Othello, under Iago's influence, also mistakes his fine manners for something darker.

Rodrigo

I have wasted myself out of my means.

Act IV Scii

Of all Iago's dupes, Rodrigo is the most pathetic. Iago strings him along, promising him success with Desdemona, even when she is married to someone else. Rodrigo hands his jewels to Iago, his money, and in the end his reputation and his life, letting himself be used to murder Cassio, but dying in the attempt.

Iago's view of Cassio
Cassio's a proper man; . . .
. . . He hath a person and a smooth dispose
To be suspected; framed to make women false.

Act I Sciii

The life and plays of Shakespeare

Life of Shakespeare

1564 William Shakespeare born at Stratford-upon-Avon.

1582 Shakespeare marries Anne Hathaway, eight years his senior.

1583 Shakespeare's daughter, Susanna, is born.

1585 The twins, Hamnet and Judith, are born.

1587 Shakespeare goes to London.

1591-2 Shakespeare writes *The Comedy of Errors*. He is becoming well-known as an actor and writer.

1592 Theatres closed because of plague.

1593-4 Shakespeare writes *Titus Andronicus* and *The Taming of the Shrew*. he is member of the theatrical company, the Chamberlain's Men.

1594-5 Shakespeare writes *Romeo and Juliet*.

1595 Shakespeare writes *A Midsummer Night's Dream*.

1595-6 Shakespeare writes *Richard II*.

1596 Shakespeare's son, Hamnet, dies. He writes *King John* and *The Merchant of Venice*.

1597 Shakespeare buys New Place in Stratford.

1597-8 Shakespeare writes *Henry IV*.

1599 Shakespeare's theatre company opens the Globe Theatre.

1599-1600 Shakespeare writes *As You Like It*, *Henry V* and *Twelfth Night*.

1600-01 Shakespeare writes *Hamlet*.

1602-03 Shakespeare writes *All's Well That Ends Well*.

1603 Elizabeth I dies. James I becomes king. Theatres closed because of plague.

1603-04 Shakespeare writes *Othello*.

1605 Theatres closed because of plague.

1605-06 Shakespeare writes *Macbeth* and *King Lear*.

1606-07 Shakespeare writes *Antony and Cleopatra*.

1607 Susanna Shakespeare marries Dr John Hall. Theatres closed because of plague.

1608 Shakespeare's granddaughter, Elizabeth Hall, is born.

1609 *Sonnets* published. Theatres closed because of plague.

1610 Theatres closed because of plague. Shakespeare gives up his London lodgings and retires to Stratford.

1611-12 Shakespeare writes *The Tempest*.

1613 Globe Theatre burns to the ground during a performance of Henry VIII.

1616 Shakespeare dies on 23 April.

Shakespeare's plays

The Comedy of Errors
Love's Labour's Lost
Henry VI Part 2
Henry VI Part 3
Henry VI Part 1
Richard III
Titus Andronicus
The Taming of the Shrew
The Two Gentlemen of Verona
Romeo and Juliet
Richard II
A Midsummer Night's Dream
King John
The Merchant of Venice
Henry IV Part 1
Henry IV Part 2
Much Ado About Nothing
Henry V
Julius Caesar
As You Like It
Twelfth Night
Hamlet
The Merry Wives of Windsor
Troilus and Cressida
All's Well That Ends Well
Othello
Measure for Measure
King Lear
Macbeth
Antony and Cleopatra
Timon of Athens
Coriolanus
Pericles
Cymbeline
The Winter's Tale
The Tempest
Henry VIII

Index

Acknowledgements
The publishers would like to thank Tom Deas and Patrick Rudd for their help in producing this book.

Picture credits
p.1 Governors of Royal Shakespeare Theatre, p.3 National Maritime Museum, London (photo Bridgeman Art Library), p.5 & 6. Peter Newark's Historical Pictures, p.9 Galleria Dell'Accademia, Venice (photo Bridgeman Art Library), p.11 Mauritshuis, The Hague (photo Bridgeman Art Library).